# HOOF TRACKS

# Tom Sharpe

Tom Sharpe Quarter Horses

1227 M ¾ Road

Loma, CO  81524

970-261-3528



Published by Arizona Cowboy Connection June 2020

This book is dedicated to my wife,

Ronna Lee Sharpe.

And to all the horses I have had the

opportunity to ride.

*Special thanks to Vess Quinlan and Sally Bates*
*for helping me to write more and better.*

# TABLE OF CONTENTS

**HORSE TRACKS**

**BROKEN TRACKS**

## FRESH TRACKS

## CAT TRACKS

# HORSE TRACKS

## Branding

Sun is lost behind the hill,
One ol' cow is bawlin' still,
Huntin' for the calf she knew was there.
Dust has settled to the ground,
Gone is all the branding sound,
Odors linger lightly in the air.

Started up before the light
Sounds of horses, out of sight,
Laying tracks to gather what they can.
Each one drops where he is told,
Pushing in what he can hold,
One would think they almost had a plan.

Ground crew setting up the pen
Big enough to hold them in,
Banging, clanging, rattling of the steel,
Pulling out the branding pot,
Light the fire, make it hot,
Tweaking all the parts to craft the deal.

Gather's done, with sense of pride,
Cows come in with calf at side
Drifting toward the trap built in the draw.
Patient now, so they don't spill
As the pen begins to fill
Imagine Charlie Russell left in awe.

Banter starts amongst the crew,
Having fun, as they will do,
Making light of work they've done before.
Dust is rising, air gets thick,
Sweaty faces, mud will stick,
Flanking calves is always such a chore.

Cultures mixed, traditions meet,
Ropes with eyes hunting feet,
Wrap or tie it solid to the horn,
Roping skills go on parade
Swing, release, a shot is made
The kind of loop from which a trap is born.

Red necked cow gets on the fight
Figured out she has the right
To add a little ruckus of her own.
Crew is scattered all around,
Perks of working on the ground,
Her attitude adjusted with a stone.

Address etched into the side
Sear the hair and burn the hide
Mark is notched into the lower ear,
Just enough to get him home
If by chance he tends roam,
Drifting off to places far and near.

Day is over, work is done,
Wishing it had just begun,
Always happens, when it finally ends.
Bellies grumble, time to eat,
Tables spread with beans and meat,
Feeding all the neighbors, family, friends.

Darkness seeps up from below,
Leaving just the evening's glow,
Stars start into filling up the night.
Cow is sounding different now,
Heard her calf and she somehow
Understands how everything is right.

## A Vision

'Cross the valley voices callin',
'Mongst the yellow leaves a-fallin',
Phantom noises vaguely in the night.
The echos keep resoundin',
Hoof beats swiftly poundin',
Specters slowly sifting into sight.

I longed for punchin' cattle,
Peaceful days astride a saddle,
With nothin' but a colt between my knees,
And once again to wander,
With time to think and ponder,
And listen to the early mornin' breeze.

Burnin' hair an' sweaty leather,
Second guessin' on the weather,
Watchin' colts a practicin' their run.
Hear a buckin' horse a squallin'
Baby calves when they're a bawlin',
Feelin' tired when a day of work is done.

Circumstance said change it,
Go out and rearrange it,
I drifted down an unfamiliar track,
'Twas there I heard the voices
Learned the burdens of my choices,
Adjusted life and earned my way on back.

### Best Account

I could give you accounts
Of jug-headed mounts,
A few of the steers I've thrown,
Loops I missed,
Girls I kissed,
Lots of the people I've known.

Of rivers I've crossed,
Spurs I have lost,
Some of the fights I had,
Of men they called boss,
A wild ol' hoss,
Things to make you real sad.

Of days when damp,
Nights in camp,
Storms as mercury fell.
Of mountains bold,
Swamps so cold,
When life too young rang a bell.

How saddles leaked,
New boots squeaked,
Ropes just wouldn't hold.
Of jobs I had,
Food gone bad,
Horses priced to be sold.

But the best of all made,
In the tracks I have laid,
The ones I treasure for sure,
Coming on at odd times
Like rhythms and rhymes,
The friendships built to endure.

### Feeding the Hogs
*(For Rod McQueary)*

As smooth as silk
Yellow kernels slide skyward
Over the fence
Taking ascending flight
Forming a perfect vertical column,
An instant of gravity defiance
Motionless in the air
Before losing to nature's pull
And dropping,
In flawless formation,
The 10-point Gold Medal winning,
Rip dive,
Into the water barrel.

And again, and again
In seamless motion
The corn rises
From the blade of Granddad's
Scoop shovel.
Every grain
In perfect pattern
Floating upward
Gliding downward,
Until the barrel is full.

Seventy years later,
I feed my horses,
Using the same swing,
Downward and backward
Forward and upward
With just the right amount of force

And timely retreat
Of tines,
To send flakes of hay
Dropping just over the fence
Into feed bunks.

And get it right,
Half the time.

## Just Past the Toe of Your Boot

Just past the toe of your boot,
Your whole life comes back to you.
All time on hold, the story is told,
All memories come into view.

Reliving your days as a child,
Toys you had in your youth,
Childhood friends, days with no ends,
A fairy that paid for your tooth.

Fights with your dad about liver,
A sister you couldn't whip,
A mulberry tree, a battered-up knee,
Horses that gave you the slip.

Miles and camps and cattle,
Places where you couldn't stay,
Lessons learned, hardships earned
A school yard where you used to play.

Faces, they are the hardest,
All of the people you'd met,
Your mother is there, the girl with dark hair,
And those that you tried to forget.

Your mind is gone from your body,
Ice has filled your veins,
No fear of the fall, no feeling at all,
No strain on your arm from the reins.

The blind bucking mare slams to a tree,
The vision no longer acute,
The creek far below, again starts to flow,
Just past the toe of your boot.

## The Round Corral

Down in Southern Colorado
    where the foothills meet the plains,
Where the mesas run on eastward,
    and it seldom ever rains,
A mile above the Purgatoire,
    full of history and ghosts,
There's a round corral of lodgepole
    and crooked cedar posts.

It was Dad and I who built it,
    back when I was only 10,
Posts were tamped in solid,
    poles laid high made up the pen.
The ground was smoothed and leveled
    where it cut into the grade
And a giant cottonwood
    would lend its cooling shade.

I spent a lot of time there
    when I was young and green,
Ridin' horses owned by others,
    turned out to be routine.
It became my place of refuge,
    to let my feelings out,
An escape from what I lived with,
    all the fear and doubt.

At first, when I was little,
    and found myself inside,
Two half Welsh ponies, small and brown,
    were set for me to ride.
It took a lot of schoolin',
    for I was young and didn't know.
So a hired hand would help me,
    to make those ponies go.

Dad would sometimes be there,
    with his rough and tumble ways,
Pushin', laughin', cussin',
    but he found no way to praise.
I only sought approval,
    just to ride those horses right,
But he had a way to scare me,
    'til I couldn't sleep at night.

It never seemed to matter
    how well I rode a colt,
Dad would always spook him,
    make him buck or bolt.
He'd laugh when I got dusted,
    said I'd never make a hand,
My spirit soon was busted,
    for I didn't understand.

It was his way of teachin' me,
    trying to make me tough,
What he did, didn't work.
    He played the game too rough.
But still I kept on ridin' 'um,
    learnin' as I went
With bigger, tougher horses,
    until my youth was spent.

I found that I could handle it,
    when I was left alone.
When someone offered help,
    it would gravel to the bone.
My anger and resentment
    ran deep back in those days,
I couldn't see reality,
    I was running in a maze.

That solid old pine round corral
    became my hiding place,
Where no one saw the many tears
    go running down my face.
I lost the fear, my anger flared,
    then I didn't care,
Any horse would suit me fine,
    as long as I was there.

I grew careless with what I rode,
    what I'd say and do,
My life had lost its meaning,
    and everybody knew.
Being old enough by then,
    to light out on my own,
I packed my truck with anger,
    and headed off alone.

Miles and camps and cattle
    took me far from home,
Figured life would turn out good,
    if I'd only roam.
But trouble was my partner
    and he wouldn't go away.
I drifted back to the round corral,
    hopin' I could stay.

It was unchanged, wouldn't work,
    felt I'd lost my mind,
A better way to spend my days
    is what I had to find.
Lookin' deep within myself,
    at resentment, anger, fear,
Why the troubles followed me,
    soon came crystal clear.

A higher stronger round corral
    was built inside of me,
It kept my feelings locked away
    where no one else could see.
When the gate was opened up,
    all these things came out,
I rode them hard, one by one,
    anger, fear and doubt.

A better life is what I made,
    the world is still unchanged,
A bitter kid is more content,
    matured and rearranged.
Years have taken youth from me,
    this I don't regret.
If it wasn't such a rugged trail,
    I wouldn't be here yet.

Someday, perhaps, my son and I
    can build a round corral,
Then we'll spend some time in there,
    he'll be my special pal,
I'd tell him of so many things,
    like troubles that I had,
And hopefully the trail he rides,
    is smoothed some by his Dad.

## Dancin'

Now, my Daddy was a dancer,
Just a high steppin' prancer,
On polished wood or asphalt covered street.
With a jug a hooch inside 'im,
An' a pretty girl beside 'im,
He could cut a jig, and really move his feet.

But the dance I most remember,
Came about just last September,
We was packin' salt, and runnin' mighty late,
Headin' out 'cross a pasture,
Not expectin' a disaster,
When Dad got down to open up the gate.

It was rainin', just a pourin',
The thunder it was roarin',
The lightnin' just a streakin' in the sky,
Dad was in a hurry,
An' he didn't have a worry,
'Til the lightin' hit a fence post way up high,

It came runnin' down the wire,
Settin' every post a fire,
'Til it reached the metal gate stick on the end,
Now Dad was holdin' tight,
It was sure a funny sight,
When his feet they took to dancin' round the bend.

He pranced her down the middle,
Bowed, an' swung her to the fiddle,
Do-si-doed, an' promenaded right back home,
Then he jitterbugged awhile,
Did the monkey right in style,
The fox trot made his feet begin to roam.

The Cotton-eyed Joe came next,
The Schottische left him vexed,
For a waltz, he was movin' right in beat,
Then the polka made him groove,
The ballet was quite a move,
An' the San Antonio Stroll was done up sweet.

Then he took to doin' the twist,
With that gate stick in his fist,
An' he did the limbo right down near the ground,
He tap danced on the grass,
The Charleston came to pass,
An' he finished with the two-step all around,

He was shakin', weak and weary,
An' his beady eyes were teary,
When I stepped right down to help him to his feet,
He was really quite a sight,
With his curly hair all white,
An' I was laughin', thinkin' it was pretty neat,

Then he cussed me good and hearty,
For not helpin' at his party,
Said I should've tried and took a chance,
I told him I was shy,
A bashful kind a guy,
Who would never try to cut in on his dance.

## The Pain

Well remembered
Is the buckskin mare
Throwing a walleyed fit
Down my spine.
Still felt is the leopard spot appy colt,
Lacking any hint of athletic ability,
Changing leads
At the wrong time.

But perhaps it was
The countless leaking saddles,
Falling horses,
80-pound bales
Which left joints popping,
Ribs and vertebrae
Too loose
To handle
Sudden moves.

## *Of Hats and Hair*

I saw her
Glance to check for privacy
Before slipping her lid
To fluff flattened flocks
And mutter non-printable words
To the mirror.

I chuckle, almost laugh
As memory recalls the comment
Made by my wife
About my "terminal case"
Of hat hair.

## Geese

I see the geese a' flying,
    winging north in perfect chevrons,
Where once I only heard them
    as they flew along their way,
They call to me, their bidding,
    to once again go with them
Awaken in a new world
    at the dawning of each day.

My heart, it wants to answer,
    move out toward the dawning,
As I listen to their pleading,
    with understanding of the truth.
I see the perfect chevrons
    winging north across the sunrise,
Knowing well my soul is bound here
    by the waning of my youth.

## Aging

When time equates to money,
    life ceases to be fun,
Each little task becomes a major chore,
Your brow collects some creases,
    the hair line fades away
Nature's way to even up the score.

The belt around your middle
    grows shorter every day,
Shirts begin to shrink across the front,
Your eyes quit picking up
    the little things they should,
Memories are elusive in the hunt.

Knees which bent so freely,
    scratching broncs, mane to tail,
Creak and pop with every grinding move.
Fingers once were nimble
    braiding ropes and reins and such,
Can barely hold on to life's roughened groove.

A half day digging post holes, stretching wire fence,
And your shoulders take a lot of heating salve.
These signs are certain evidence
    you're taking on some age,
Just souvenirs of the life you used to have.

But would you trade the present
    for more trips down the trail?
Think before you answer yes or no.
It wasn't quite as pretty
    as the stories you often tell,
Scars are all you seem to have to show.

Mornings when you rolled out
    for the pre-dawn breakfast bell
To fork some bronc you knew you couldn't trust.
Would set your stomach stewin'
    'til you couldn't eat a thing
Wonderin' if he'd dump you in the dust.
The winter in Wyoming,
      the cows near starved to death,
Awful tough to listen to 'em bawl.

The flu took your horses,
    there was nothing you could do
But sit and listen to the Master call.
The thought of mother's chicken,
    mashed potatoes, apple pie,
Laid out on a table, what a sight.
Compared to bungled biscuits
    and a bowl of boiled beans,
To set your belly rumbling in the night.

Damn, it sure got lonely
    in those camps up in the hills,
The only face you saw was in the mirror.
Seemed the world forgot you,
    left without a care,
You sometimes saw your mother once a year.
Broken bones and bruises
    and those eighteen hour days,
It wasn't as romantic as portrayed.
Still you rode for wages
    at the only thing you knew,
Times you wonder why you ever stayed.

Now your saddle's getting dusty,
    perched up in the barn,
Swapped it for a swivel seat in town,
Bits and spurs are hanging
    with your chaps there on a peg,
You wonder if you'll ever take them down.

All you have is memories
    mincing in your muddled mind,
And feelings which are seldom understood.
Though time has taken tally
    on the many things you've done,
You'd go back in a minute if you could.

### It Can Happen in An Instant
*(For Dusty)*

It can happen in an instant,
    'bout as fast as lightning, greased,
Or come on fairly, slowly,
    as if time and motion ceased,
No matter of the tempo,
    the forecast is never great,
For circumstance has interfered,
    transformed receiver's fate.

A hand gets quickly tangled up
    'twixt horn and dally rope,
An arm becomes the landing gear
    from dog hole at a lope,
A cow somehow hits a gate,
    a wrist takes all the smash,
A baling string gets frozen down,
    fingers take the crash.

Talking sailor comes on natural,
    no way to curb the tongue,
As pain removes good instinct
    and all manners get far flung.
Anguish must be pushed aside,
    when bones regain the feeling,
A spell will pass before the breaks
    begin at slowly healing.

An ill-timed trip down to the town,
    becomes the next in sequence,
Hopefully this type of thing
    is not of too much frequence.
Plates of steel, screws and pins,
    a doctor's tender mending,

Savings plan, built over time,
    has reached the day for spending.

The major chores will soon get done,
    cows require feeding,
And clearly all the other stock,
    will not be left in needing.
But smaller stuff steps in the way,
    the "how to" takes some trying,
And dauntingly, there are some things,
    at first, seem quite defying.

The soup spoon just won't hit the hole
    and get to where it's going,
And down the front of nice clean shirt,
    a cup of coffee's flowing.
Boots are tight, when fitting right,
    not made for one side tugging,
Bigger things are not quite built
    for single handed lugging.

Snaps are not too tricky,
    with two fingers, if in line,
Buttons take a little more
    of digit bending time.
Zippers can be easy,
    when lined up good and straight,
Cutting steak, with one hand,
    takes on a different fate.

Shaving is a problem,
    with a razor to the throat,
Getting arms into the sleeves
    of favorite heavy coat.

Washing hand is not quite grand,
    the tendency, to wipe it,
Pen and paper will not work,
    better off to type it.

Brushing teeth, the mirror reveals,
    a funny type of pace,
Toothbrush held in one good hand,
    and yes and no the face,
But hardest of the many tricks,
    contorting for the caper,
Of mastering required skill
    with left-hand toilet paper.

# BROKEN TRACKS

**2002**

2:00 AM, June 3.
Pilled-up mind stays wide awake
While cast-sore leg aches
From bone snapping horse-cow run-in
10 days ago.


**Pain**

Hip high cast
Causes sleep starved nerves
To SCREAM
At little brown bottle
Of little white pills
For relief.

## Sassy

A dream summer of colts and travel,
Evaporated when panicked mare exploded.
She hit a half a dozen cows
While jumping, kicking through 50 feet of searing nylon.
Stopping, she asked what she had done
To earn such a burn?
Easing Paul Bond from oxbow
To release pressure on newly formed joints,
I rubbed her mane,
Knowing the leg went on the first jump,
And I had no answer for her question.

## One Wonders

One wonders if folks ever think,
When eyeing hip to toe cast
And their first question is:
"Did you fall off your horse?"

You may as well answer up "yes"
For it takes too long to explain
How these prizes aren't given away free.


## The Easy Chair

Just the thought
of being 4 months
a-butt-back,
Speeds chills down spine.
Why couldn't it have been
a-horse-
or at worst,
a-foot-?


## Down For The Count

Being a-butt-back,
Is like being a-foot-back,
Only worse.

## The Farmer

He talked about being a good farmer,
Having raised tons of great alfalfa,
How agriculture had once been
    the mainstay of his life.
The two toppled stack-hand loads of hay left doubts.
But doubts became knowledge,
    when they were left that way,
And the hay molded.
I wonder if the expensive new houses he now builds
Are any better.

## Windmills

Western Kansas roots
Inspires my wife's interest
In windmills.
She collects them.
Wooden, metal and glass miniatures,
Pictures on canvas, leather, wood and saw blades,
All kinds of windmills adorn our house.

But one night,
High on pain relief,
I pulled a modern day Don Quixote
And mowed down twelve of them
With my Tommy-Crutch.

## Crashed Again

Trying to make one more good 'un
Coaxing maturity,
From a gangly 4-year-old
With no "wait and see"
And a "rather play" attitude.

He scattered.
Gravity trumped balance
Legs and feet tangled
Crashing into fence
Going down, up, and down again,
Leaving me Raggedy Ann'ed
At ground level.

Memory stopped recording,
As knots replaced temple,
Twisted mangled lower limb
Formed new joints,

Recall rebooted with lower limb pain,
Breathing more dirt than air,
Being held down, rolled over,
Loaded and hauled out.
Shirt, pants and another Paul Bond,
Relinquished their jobs to scissors.

Three days of nurses, surgery,
12 new screws, more titanium,
(I am worth a lot now, titanium is pricey)
And Mitch said,
Next time,
He'd just weld me back together.

## The Player

There are two kinds.
Players and spectators
Those who sit the fence
And those in the corral.

But don't you think
14 inches of titanium,
12 more screws,
Knee to toe cast,
Two broken ribs,
A concussion,
Lots of knots
And bruises,
Are a mite much,
For a participation award?

## Busted

"I'm really good with crutches"
Is a testament to a skill
Earned from a total lack of talent.

## Keeping Score

Can you count one leg
Broke in four places
At one time,
As four broken legs?

## Medicine Bag

Not unlike the medicine bag
I packed for years
Made from a cut-off boot top,
Snapped and strapped snug
Behind my leg,
Packing enough drugs to doctor
20 head of yearlings,
Combiotic, Sulfa pills, I-Ball,
syringes, needles, balling gun
Roping on "affordable" horses,
Riding 30-mile circles.

The four-inch canvas tote,
The kind given away as advertising,
Now swings from my walker,
On my 12-foot treks
As I do the horrible hobble
Between bed and bathroom
Packing my cell phone.

## Sometimes

There are times
When mind trumps
Pills and pain,
Hiding sleep,
In places I won't go.

It grabs the bits
Kicks over the traces
And has a full-fledged runaway,
Romping and stomping
Through mountains and valleys
Of should'ves and could'ves and would'ves,
Loping with might'ves and might nots, and maybes,
Seeking solutions to problems not there.
Loosing the worry and masses of wonder
To ponder and wander
Through canyons and gorges
Of gloom and despair.

Sanity slowly slips into its traces,
Tugging the light of more rational thought,
Revealing the value of all of that racing,
Knowing full well of the waste of the time.

And sleep comes,
Slipping softly serenely
Sincerely.

## Butt Bound and Bored

As pretty as posies
My Houlihan'd paracord loop
With 5 coils
Settles around a water bottle
Perched on dresser's edge
10 feet away.

And you'd thought I'd roped a bear,
The way my wife offered
To take my rope away
As she released my catch
For the third time.

# GATHERING TRACKS

## The Gathering

*(For all the Duleys and Donnies and Emilys*
*who got sorted and culled)*

They found us in our teepees, camps
    or hidden in the closet
Penning words 'bout what we do or did.
Hiding from the outer world,
    not trusting in ourselves,
Kinda like a stomped on little kid.

We stuffed 'um in an empty jar
    and hid 'um in the rafters,
The whys of which we didn't understand.
And if we ever pulled one out
    to see the light of day,
'Twas only 'mongst disciples of our band.

But they asked us sort of kindly,
    come and share of the tradition,
Enjoy the "works" of others of your kind,
So we went and brought our secrets,
    from their many years of hiding,
Curious 'bout the types and things we'd find.

We'd known of each other, kinda, sorta,
    somewhat, maybe,
Never met before, but friends for many years,
Bonds were formed within our band,
    friends solidified,
'Til parting often left us all in tears.

Outsiders came to see us,
    with no knowledge of the working,
Believing they could live the cowboy dream.
And with them came the money,
    fueling fires built for fanning,
Forming up a different type of scheme.

'Twas then the judging started,
         placing one above another,
The trophy buckle offered as a prize.
The sights of lights and microphones,
      the stage where egos stand,
Unmindful of traditions 'fore their eyes.

Soon ego took the spotlight
      for the mighty silver dollar,
Often one would ride afore the rest.
The code that we had lived by,
      taught us by our elders,
Lost amongst attempts to be the best.

And some of them within us,
      ignored the rules we followed,
Forfeiting the way of life they knew,
Chasing after lights and silver,
      seeking fame and glory,
Discarding of the code they once held true.

Then others came to join them,
      who knew not cowboy culture,
Drawn to the silver and the stage.
And they pushed aside the real ones,
      left them standing in the aisle,
And stole the very essence, for the wage.

Those who lacked the ego,
      holding strong to the tradition,
Didn't care for lights and silver and the stage,
So the true in spirit drifted,
      back to the camps and teepees,
And the best is safely hid amid the sage.

# DIVERGING TRACKS

# Twenty One Years Later

(Vietnam)

A careless step
And a bad bull
Kept me from the war.

I saw a different war.
One of protestors
Burning flags and buildings.
Rioting,
Unreasonable,
Ungrateful.

I watched as the Ag Building
Was seized in protest.
A six year graduate study
Ruined.

I saw flames
Turn Old Main
To ashes.

I saw young men
Disown their country,
Forsake family and friends.

I was grateful
For freedom of speech.
Disgusted
By what they said.

It hurt to see
Friends return,
Bodies and minds
Broken.

I was incensed
When our Nation
Refused
To honor them.

It haunts me still.
Could I have made a difference?
Would my name be on The Wall
Instead of Gary's?

## Land Use Planning Math

It takes fewer farms
To fabricate fifty homes
On 5-acre sites
Than on quarter-acre lots.


## On Conservation Easements

Conservation easements
Preserve agriculture
About as often
As I win the lottery.


## Mountain Top Trophy Homes

More about seen,
Than scene.


## Untitled

She said leave
Disappear
Pretend this never happened

So I left
Disappeared
And tried to pretend
It never happened.

## Recycling

Raised by parents
Whose parents
Survived "The Great Depression",
We have become a generation
Of "Save-Its".
We save everything
From Spotted Owls
To never-heard-of-before plants.
From the ozone layer to the ocean floor,
Recycle is a way of life.

But my mind was baffled,
Plumb stupefied
By the whys and hows
Leading to the printing
Of "100% Recycled"
On a package
Of toilet paper.

## Congress 2019

Sheep trailing the Judas goat,
Of old ego and personal agenda,
With no independent thought
Of where or what or who.
The noise of inexperience
Forming nonsensical solutions
To serious situations
Crowding the sides and pushing the drag
Toward the inevitable cliff
Of no return.

# 9/11/16

I sit and watch
A replay of what happened
Fifteen years ago today

The horrific attack
On our nation.
Our nation
Where we live.

I watched for days
As our people pulled together
Unified in a way
We had not seen
In sixty plus years.

I watched
As flags were flown
As the Pledge of Allegiance
Was recited by everyone
Often.

I watched
As we became
The United States of America
Again.

Today,
I watch the replay
Disturbed by
How quickly we forgot.

## Remains

Dad fought in the Second,
Told stories
Of bombing flights over Europe
And how Axis Sally
Knew more than he did.
Joked about tending bar
In a London pub
During air raids.
Laughed about Russian ladies
Carrying him to a dance,
When he was too tired
To go.

Spoke of how they were shot down
Over Vienna
While on a recon mission.
Armed with a forty-five
And five bullets.
Three for the camera,
One each for them.
He and the pilot, named White,
Walked to the tip of Italy
From behind enemy lines,
Hid in basements, and didn't bathe
For eighty-nine days.

Years later White died
Under a car
In New York traffic.
Dad came home terrified
To be alone.
Built nightly veils
With alcohol
And sleeping pills
To shelve
The untold stories.

# Time to Stay Home

*(Afghanistan)*

Life is some confusing at times,
As our boys again load and leave
To help humanity
And feed the hungry people
In another land.

This time to a drought ridden nation
Whose own people
Won't allow their own
To be fed
With food sent by more prosperous peoples.

I sit and wonder
About many things
Like why do we always go
To help?
Why are all the world problems
Ours to solve?
Don't we have enough to do here
Can't we allow our boys to stay home
For Christmas
And rebuild cities
Ravaged by summer storms
And riots?

Yes, I think it is time
For us to stay home,
Work on some of what is bothering us here
And let some of the rest of the world
Work on their own problems.

## Growing Up

Making good decisions
Comes from experience
Suffering the consequences
Of bad decisions.

Failure to allow failure
And bear the results
Initiates the illusion
Of being gifted
With imaginary knowledge and skill.

## Passions

By the time I turned twelve,
Dad was convinced
There were three things
I would never learn to do:
Run a tractor, irrigate
And work cows a-foot.

## Out of Shame
(Gulf War)

Yellow ribbons
Live news coverage
Everyone hoping
The war will end
Soon.
Hoping sons
And daughters
will return safely.

Fathers of the young troops
Talk of the last war,
Their war.
When a nation
Shamed itself
By not honoring
Them.

# FRESH TRACKS

## School

Little plastic pistol grips
    in holsters on his slender hips
Riding broncy footstool for a score,
Dressed in chaps and dime store hat,
    red felt vest, blue cravat,
It made him want to cowboy all the more.

He'd get bucked off, get back on,
    worked at it dawn to dawn,
Instilling in his mind this cowboy rule,
He longed to find a better ride,
    until he did it's footstool snide
He studied hard, at his cowboy school.

Cowboys from the little screen
    fanned the flames of child's dream
Teaching of the code that won the West.
Roy and Gene and Hopalong
    always seemed to come along
To prove to all how right is always best.

A favorite horse they always rode,
    one more lesson from the code,
Another's horse is his alone to ride,
Never ever dodge a fight,
    but only if you know you're right,
The good guys always will be at your side.

A cotton rope was his to use,
    practice hard, don't abuse,
He learned to build a loop and swing it too.
Anything that came his way,
    if it moved, it was prey
And in his mind he always heard it moo.

Time is always moving past,
     going on until at last,
He's trotting out a horseback 'crost the land
Simple lessons he had learned,
     right of passage he had earned,
His dream come true amidst a cowboy band.

# The Cow

*(For Beeman Casto)*

I reckon I will keep her
    for she's not the shipping kind,
And she's earned the right to live here on this range.
We've built a bond between us,
    respect and understanding,
Yeah, it comes across to most as being strange.

She's not the family pet by far,
    has never earned a name,
Best step aside when she comes trotting through,
But she'll lead a bunch to better grass
    and find a water hole
When gentle cows just don't know what to do.

I remember her first calving
    in the willows by the creek,
How she grieved the death for 5 straight days and nights.
She still tends that sacred spot
    when down from summer hills,
And as she wants, I guess it is her right.

She brings a calf in every fall,
    just doing her fair share,
For we really need the banker held at bay,
It seems she owns a part of this,
    at least she thinks she does,
And it surely isn't mine to have a say.

So, we keep on going forward,
    hunting grass and better times,
Making do with what we come across each day,
And I know I'll never change it,
    not even if I could,
'Til the sound of greener grass calls us away.

## Blue Eyes

"You're not a cowboy!"

I looked around to see who made the remark and saw a shiny pair of new boots wearing a big black hat. A pair of blue eyes stared up at me from under the brim. He looked tough. Too tough for me to tangle with. So I just said, "Yep."

"Cowboys don't wear caps!"

"Nope."

"Cowboys have ropes."

"Yep."

"Cowboys ride horses.  I have a horse."

"You do? Where you from, partner?"

"I ain't your partner."

"Yep."

"You a farmer? I don't like farmers."

"Nope."

"Joey, come here! Leave the man alone."

I glanced around to see what pretty voice had bumped into our conversation, and found another pair of blue eyes, just like the ones under the brim of Joey's hat.

"Hi, Sam, how are you?"

"Mommy, do you know him?"

"Hush, Joey."

I still didn't know what to say. It had been a while, maybe too long, too many miles. Maybe I should have stayed. Too many maybes.

"Heard you were in Wyoming."

"Yep."

"When did you get back?"

"Couple of weeks ago."

"Gonna be around for awhile?"

"I dunno."

"Call me, will you? You still have the number."

"OK." I lied.

I wouldn't call.

It was easier to talk to Joey. She knew it.

What went wrong? Who knows, and now it didn't matter. She was still in my mind. I hadn't been able to outrun that.

It was better now, well, it had been.

Why'd she have to show up and open the gate on the memories?

Joey sure is a cute kid, and I bet it was hard on him when his daddy left. Don't know about that either. At least it wasn't me that left them.

But I had left.

Maybe I would call.

Maybe.

## Changes

Pulling calves,
Feeding hay,
Very seldom
Time to play.

Patching up
Pickup truck,
Pulling out
Bull that's stuck.

Mowing down
Summer hay,
Winter time
Fed away.

Poor ol' cows
Mighty thin.
Air is cold,
Against the skin.

Job in town,
Pay is low,
Need the money,
To make it go.

"Money tight",
Bankers say.
Grandpa's ranch
Sold today...

## Customs

A lifetime of cows and horses
Left the cowman wizened to the ways of trades
    and traders,
And proud of his proficiency
In obtaining the best of the deal.

When luck found him and his spouse of 30 years
In the Land of Sand along the northern shores of Africa,
He found his trading skills and quick humor challenged.
As allowed by Moroccan custom,
5 camels were offered for his wife.
Winking at his bride, he quickly replied
"50 Camels."
Surprise turned to fear when the turban topped trader,
Seizing the woman by the arm,
Agreed to the deal.

## The Ol' Man and the Lady

Ol' man's got his dander up,
Howlin' like a fool,
Roarin', screamin', all about,
Seems to be his rule.

He's moody and destructive
Always apt to fight,
No one seems to like his
Wailin', day and night.

Temper gets the best of him,
Then he's on a spree,
Rompin', stompin', throwin' things
Scatterin' debris.

He's married to a lady,
An easy flowin' bride,
So soothin' when she's singin',
But never by his side.

No one ever seems to mind
When she comes driftin' by,
Whisperin' such a gentle song
That sounds 'most like a sigh.

Makes you wonder how this pair
Stay married with such ease,
Different, yet alike somehow
Ol' Man Wind and Lady Breeze.

## Talk

Folks claim
To preserve the past,
Cling to the old ways,
Use time-honored grandfather-taught skills.

Yet,
Hay is machine stacked,
Calf cradles smash fingers,
And horses are bought broke.

## Sweat

Working hard
For wages
Seeing the fruit of labor,
And feeling tired at day's end
Is the mainstay of life
For those who work the land.
Countless postholes,
and bales of hay
Sculpted shoulders
Thinned waist
Defined muscles.

Today
I question my own sanity
And that of other 9 to 5ers
Who don Reeboks at daybreak
Nikes at noon
Or Adidas after five
Then hit the asphalt,
To stay trim and fit.
And waste
Sweat.

## Women's Lib

The three silver-haired sisters
Rode along in comfortable companionship.
It had been many years
Since they were girls
Working together on the ranch.
Today they moved their brother's
Retirement herd of 70 head
Six miles between summer pastures
While their brother
Lazily followed along in the pickup.

A young neighbor
Spied the women,
Stopped to visit a spell
Then moved on to speak
To their brother.

"Crafts," said the neighbor,
"I never thought I'd see the day
When you'd be working
A whole crew of women."

"Bill" replied Crafts,
"I've been waiting a long time
For this day."

## Mornin'

Sweet
Neat
Little feet
Patterin' 'crost the floor,

Deep
Sleep
Now complete,
Rattlin' at the door.

## The Window

Settled, alone, quietly in the corner,
Aged, weathered, sipping coffee.
Unnoticed, except by a pretty waitress
Silently, refilling his cup.

He stares out the window,
Longingly, misty eyed.

The grand old ranch where he herded
Starts at the edge of town,
A quarter of a million acres, from valley floor
To snow-capped peaks.

Watches the valley where he wintered,
Knows lambing pens
Hidden from view.
The summer range,
High mountain meadows,
Still covered with late snow.

Miles of road scar the piñon hills,
Connecting scattered houses.
No sheep, no cows, no cowboys, no herders.
Just memories.

He stares out the window.

## The Drifter

More miles and horses than he cared to remember
An outfit a year, three wives and several saddles
Left him broke, alone and traveling.
As a young man he dreamed of settling
On a place of his own,
Finding someone to share it with
And leaving it all to his son.
But whiskey, broncs and women
And the insatiable urge to wander
Left him standing on the side of the road
Waiting for a place to go.

## The King

Just a common kind of cowboy
    on his way from now 'til then,
Never spending too much thinking
    On what could or should have been,
Enjoying all the freedom drawing wages will allow,
An' gaining world perspective
    looking lengthwise through a cow.

Never saving too much money
    but enough to meet the need,
Never placing any value upon power, fame, or greed,
With uncanny hands he handles horses,
    a divinely granted knack,
And he leaves a trail behind him
    where he's always welcome back.

## Thoughts

There have been a lot of stories 'bout the romance
    of the cowboy
The hired man a horseback being king.
'Til it blowed plumb out of reason,
    getting into cowboy heads
Thoughts of self-importance set to wing.

The fencer and the farmer, the windmill and the hay
No one beats ol' cousie and his chow.
The hoodlum and the wrangler
    doing chores and other things,
Equally important to the cow.

So climb down off the pedestal
    and recognize your worth,
The hat you wear is not a fabled crown.
Better hands are hard to find,
    but they dang shore won't be worse
Respect those folks a-working on the-ground.

## The Vigil

She stayed
For five days
With her still-born calf.

Driven to another pasture
She fed briefly and drank hard
Before returning
Through seven fences in two hours
To guard and grieve
As she worked out the loss
Of her first-born.

# $50 Boot

In the Deep South
At the edge of the Okefenokee Swamp
Lived a horse and mule dealer
Who wanted Grandpa Leonard's
Little gray driving mare.
Hitched to the surrey on Sundays,
The mare was Grandpa Leonard's pride and joy.
Over the years,
Repeated attempts at a swap
Left the trader
Frustrated in failure.

The morning after the mare died,
With knees locked,
Propped against a distant tree,
The horse and mule dealer happened by.
For two sound mules
And $50 boot,
Grandpa Leonard
Proudly made the trade.

## Granny and Her Knittin'

Granny and her knittin',
    slowly rockin' to and fro,
Building socks for all those people,
    she knew so long ago,
The clicking of her needles
    keeping pace with memories' flow
As her mind begins its driftin'
    back to times she used to know.

Ranch raised up in a country
    where the rabbits lugged a lunch,
Where rainfall was of short supply
    then came all in a bunch.
If scenery was an asset,
    they would have owned a bank,
Edges, ledges, canyon walls,
    to make those horseshoes clank.

Learning chores when she was little,
    until old enough to ride,
She yearned to be a horseback,
    not left at mother's side.
She didn't mind the housework,
    but would rather be outside,
Leaving with the sunrise,
    hunting cows on some ol' snide.

She gained the reputation
    of being wizened to the cow,
The whys and wheres and whens to her,
    came natural somehow.
The mysteries of their hidden trails,
    their ways off every rim
To secret spots of greener grass

where tracking got real dim.
She studied at her horses
    'til she understood their ways,
With some it came so easily,
    with others it took days.
The softer and the slower,
    the better were the plays,
Always asking, never taking,
    gentle hands, is how it pays.

Time came she owned the outfit,
    living out there all alone,
Tending to the life she loved
    and to the seeds she'd sown.
But life, it waits for no one,
    it is always on the go,
But Granny's got her knitting,
    slowly rocking to and fro.

## The Boss

He was slow to meet the gather,
    but he brought a decent jag,
Coming in from country no one rode,
The cowboys all took notice
    as he dropped into a spot,
Riding up to ease the others' load.

No one made a comment,
    but they snickered to themselves
As they eyed this new addition to the crew.
But he was soon forgotten,
    with Shorty in there sorting,
The work they had was all that they could do.

And when the work was over,
    the cut punched through a gate,
The boys began to visit and to share.
But the stranger held his distance,
    didn't join in with the others
As Shorty trotted out to meet him there.

The boys took in to laughing
    'bout the stranger and his rig,
The saddle that he rode was way too small,
His brogan shoes and bibbers,
    the floppy holey hat,
The jacket didn't seem to fit at all.

A cotton rope, a bridle rein,
    a bailing twine the other.
Headstall held together with a string,
The mule he came a riding on,
    had seen some better days,
His single spur had passed its time to sing.

Shorty turned and headed back,
     the stranger rode away,
The questions from the crew would fill a book.
He said "he owns this outfit,
     and two more just as good,
And really can't afford the cowboy look."

## Hard Tracks

Years have etched the miles
    in the canyons of his face,
Fingers gnarled and twisted,
    his back set in a brace,
His mind got stuck at thirty,
    his body eighty-five.
All things told, I reckon,
    he is lucky he's alive.
He'd gone to school just long enough
    to learn to read and write
And always figured better things
    were just beyond his sight.
He'd taken up the cowboy trade,
    it let him move around,
Freedom was his calling,
    he was always outward bound.
He plied his skills wherever
    he could find a horse and cow
And always left before he had
    the chance to learn to plow.
But years were in a long trot,
    bringing on impending truth,
Leaving tracks between the now,
    and where he left his youth.
His body finally gave it up
    and stuck him in a chair,
Wheels became his only means
    to get from here to there.
His memory got all shuffled,
    simply muddled up in time,

He's living in the moment,
    back when he was in his prime.
He saddled up this morning,
    headed out for Chico Flat,
He's tending to some heifers there,
    on brome and winterfat.
Yesterday was Brush Creek,
    he summers yearlings there.
Before, it was a calving job,
    then Elko County Fair.
He's starting colts in Weston,
    hunting mavericks on the Blue,
Packing salt to Winter Camp,
    then branding with the crew.
Some morning he will saddle-up
    the horse that no one knows
And ride out for the country
    where the unleashed spirit goes.
He'll start again to drifting,
    go to trotting 'cross the land
Where freedom for his soul is found
    within a cowboy band.

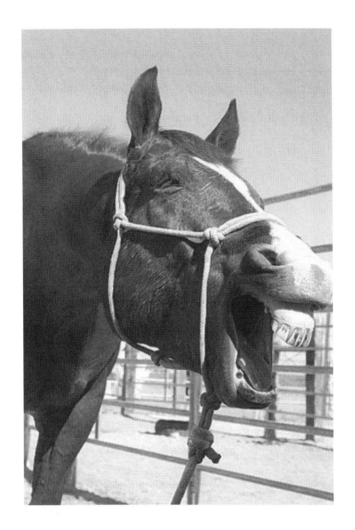

# CAT TRACKS

## 4-H Cat Project

Trent, I was glad to see 4-H finally decided to offer a cat project. I would be a good leader for this and feel I would have a lot to offer in the survival skills area of the project.

Things every cat should know, like how to avoid the neighbor's dog, how to procure food on your own, living on the minimum, building a hay stack shelter plan, ignoring humans (I'm a good one to ignore), dealing with foxes, avoiding air strikes from owls and hawks and why not to sleep by the truck's radiator.

Artful things, like leaving fur balls on the bathroom floor, how to open the toilet for a drink, furniture marking with claws, claw rug exercises and sleeping on the recliner. Fun things like, shedding where it is least appropriate, toe pouncing from under the bed, counter hopping, mouse chasing in the bathtub, leaving squeaky toys in the hall at night, and my personal favorite, table hopping during dinner.

Every cat could improve on skills like tripping people carrying eggs, sleeping in the laundry basket, not coming when called and having kittens on the new bedspread.

This project would tie in well with the gerbil project and a joint exercise program could be worked out for the two of them.

A catch-a-cat contest is a possibility involving the county animal control officers, with quantity not quality being the deciding factor.

We could work out an agility course for them and include things like getting stuck in a glass jar, public body part cleaning, venetian blind climbing, Christmas tree tipping, ornament batting, curtain shredding and shelf climbing. The list is endless.

Yes, I think I would make a great cat project leader.

## My Wife Had a Cat

My wife had a cat. I moved in with them. All of us are at fault for this story.

I had been living on a mountain, 9,000 feet up, 2 ½ miles from my closest neighbor, where coyotes woke me, chipmunks were my pets and pack rats my nemesis. 90% of my time was spent alone, in quiet solitude, listening to and enjoying nature all night. I lost interest in working where I was, so I came up with a better plan, and moved to town, with a woman who had a cat.

Moving from an isolated log house, occupied by me and a couple of pack rats, to town, into an apartment complex, on a very busy street with cars, sirens, motorcycles, heart stressing stereos and a cat snoring on the pillow was truly culture shock. I didn't sleep. Nobody slept. Nerves grew tight, tempers tighter. The cat didn't sleep.

The cat wasn't trainable; spending time alone, sleeping in another room, weren't good options, the howling, the scratching, the "I ain't going to be alone and I liked my life better before you" attitude really didn't help. Nothing helped. I didn't sleep.

But this cat had redeeming habits. Looking hard at making 20, she liked to play, would invent things to do. One time for a birthday, I bought an aluminum helium filled balloon. The ribbon hung down to about two feet off the floor, higher than the cat could reach standing on hind legs. She jumped, batted the ribbon, caught it in her mouth and left. This apartment was u-shaped, kitchen, dining area, living area, hall, bedrooms. The cat took off trailing the balloon along, bouncing it off of walls and furniture from living room down the hall, over the bed, back down the hall, through the living room, around the dining table, into the kitchen, around the table, through the living room, down the hall, over the bed, etc. Not once, but until she got tired, 30 minutes or more at a time. She wore out the balloon. She wore out another balloon, and another. Like food and water, the cat had to have her balloon.

This cat was noisy, talked to anyone who would talk back, and probably understood all that was being said. I had to be careful so as not to say things that I didn't want repeated. It was as bad as living with a three-year old, repeating everything said.

She liked peacock feathers, would play with them until whoever was playing with her got tired or the feather wore out. Anything that moved was fair game, drag a string, roll a ball, anything.

We got married (not me and the cat), didn't ask the cat, still she just tolerated me. My new wife traveled a lot for business. She loved her cat and liked me. I was under threat of life or worse, to take care of the cat. We moved, found a couple of acres with a house, got away from the traffic, and I could sleep. One day while my wife was gone, I was in charge of the cat, like feed, water, litter box, safety, health and welfare. I got ready to go to work and couldn't find the cat. I checked beds, under the beds, closets and cabinets, stove, trash can, no cat. I went back through the house, again, and again. No cat. I knew I had better pay my insurance up, and start digging, 'cause the cat got out and I was dead. This declawed cat had never set foot outside, knew nothing of trees and bushes and neighborhood dogs. I was dead. I hadn't been out that day, so the cat had been gone overnight. Making another tour of the house, I, by chance, glanced into the second bathroom, and a head popped up, out of the bathtub. Maybe, I wasn't dead. There she was, sitting on the drain. Backed up on the other end of the tub was a very still mouse. Wow, cat had caught a mouse and killed it. I reached over to pick up the dead mouse and it took off, circled the cat and ran up the slope, slid back and played dead. The cat watched. I touched the mouse, the mouse ran, the cat batted the mouse, the mouse slid up the bathtub wall and back down, played dead. This game, without me, must have been going on for a spell, and soon the mouse took its last at bat and went to wherever mice go when they take their last at bat. I dumped the mouse. The cat took a nap. I went to work.

Time expresses its control over all things. And cats, even with their famous nine lives, are still affected by it. The cat wore out. Age, miles and the total number of times the cat was petted, took their toll. The cat went to where mice don't have a "last at bat," where balloons don't wear out, and there are no limits on the number of times they can be petted.

Arizona
Cowboy
Connection

Publishings of
Sally Harper Bates